Welch Doctrine

BY GREGORY WELCH

DORRANCE
PUBLISHING CO
EST. 1920
PITTSBURGH, PENNSYLVANIA 15238

Dorrance Publishing Co
585 Alpha Drive
Suite 103
Pittsburgh, PA 15238
Visit our website at *www.dorrancebookstore.com*

ISBN: 978-1-6495-7215-8
eISBN: 978-1-6495-7723-8

Welch Doctrine

Acknowledgements

To my mother, who has stayed with me through the struggle through thick and thin. Amir Ali, for being there when needed the most. James T. Dawson, the years have flown by, it seems as if you were there the entire time. Lindsay Harrison, thank you for being a blessing to me! To the entire staff at Jenner & Block, I appreciate you 100%. To the Public Defenders in the Florida Southern District and all over America, who work selflessly to help the helpless, who thrive to bridge the gap, and to the people who feel they cannot achieve anything. Please believe anything is possible. To the individuals that helped the Welch Doctrine to be possible. Twin a.k.a. Norris Williams, my brother Unique, Tyson, Jungle, Wee, Stone, Joseph Martin. I would like to personally thank Henry Lousi Gates, Malcolm Gladwell, and all the authors who helped shed light when things seemed hopeless. To the staff, who believed in me when no one else did. To the people who never thought that I would get it right. It's all love. It was needed because Frederick Douglass said it best: "There can never be progress without struggle." Last but not least, thank you to everyone who turned their back.

Thank you.

I

I arrived at F.C.C. Coleman Medium on June 13, 2013. I was transferred from the United States Penitentiary #2, within the Federal Correctional Complex, Coleman, Florida. It was a very hot day. I was taken out from the Pen-Two (as it is called) because I had low points. The Region (Regional Director's staff) came through and started selecting people to be removed from behind the walls of higher security institutions. I was one of the individuals to be removed. I was upset because I felt I was taken out of my comfort zone. Being there seemed surreal but it was a world within itself. I was looking forward to getting my 2255 done. A 28 U.S.C. § 2255 is what you file after your conviction becomes final. Your conviction is final when the Supreme Court would either grant or deny certiorari review and from that date the clock starts to run, meaning you have one year from the actual date of denial to file a 28 U.S.C. § 2255. My certiorari was denied on January 7, 2013, the cite was 568 U.S. 1112. I started to pay attention to my case more when I went to the Supreme Court the first time, I felt that my issue was misplaced. The meaning of misplaced is when the argument or briefs are not litigated properly (yes, I am really saying that).

When I got to the Medium I was living in B-1 Housing Unit, was told to live in Cell 34 which was a TV cell. I did not care for TV too much. I was always either reading law or reading different periodicals on law. The irony behind it is that I look like I am straight out of a prison movie, tattooed up, tall and dark skin. My cellie was an older Jamaican, he was an old-school Spangler. He said he knew my family and that we had supporters and rivals here. I told him I am not into anything. Where is the law library? What classes can I take? I told him I was into Suicide Watch, and he laughed and he said, "Since when does Welch care about not putting someone in the grave!" I said, "It's whatever you want to think then."

He took me around to the different departments. I was always a loner so I did not care to meet anyone. I would eat by myself and sometimes talk to some people occasionally but small talk. I was introduced to Stone, who taught the legal research class. I signed up for the class then. When I showed up, it was like the beginning of the end; it started off with 25 people, then it dwindled down to about 7. Stone was self-assured we would always bump heads. The real lessons were after class, he would sit me down and always tell me that I was very intelligent and that I was going to be successful, and he said he did not know why he was saying it but it was something that had to be said. I am grateful to Stone for having extra talks after class. I learned about case cites, I would memorize the cases he would give me to read and the year the cases were decided. For instance, in a United States Supreme Court Reporter, Crawford v. Washington 541 U.S. 36 (2004) specifically talks about the confrontation clause which is the right to confront your accusers and how you could lose it—explained in Melendez-Diaz v. Massachusetts 557 U.S. 305 (2009). I knew my direct appeal is United States v. Welch 683 F.3d 1211 (2012). The cite is like your phone number in the legal world. I used to compare it to your slave number. I learned on my own that federal cases become a part of history. You have cases that are published and cases that are not published. Published cases have either a current Federal Reporter, third series number or they look like this: 123 (volume) F.3d 456 (page numbers) or like this: (second series) 123 F.2d 456. Whenever I would see F.2d, I know that they are normally older cases. Older appellate cases are good when you want to show an established constitutional right that has never been changed. For instance, in ex parte Siebold 100 U.S. 371 (1880), the U.S. Supreme Court case addressed why substantive rules must have retroactive effect regardless of when the defendant's conviction became final.

I was sentenced on September 17, 2010, for felony possession of a firearm. My sentence became final on January 7, 2013, when the Supreme Court denied my certiorari. When I was taking the legal research class, Stone asked me when I was going to file my 2255, at that time I did not know how to file a

2255. I was hanging with Ish and he kept saying I should go to "Stoney" because he was the homie (homie in Federal prison means someone from the same area where your from or someone who knows you) and he had been down for a long time and knew what he was doing (I felt differently, though). Stone would have classes with me on Saturdays. I would break down cases in the Supreme Court, historical data, years they came out, who wrote the dissent, why the dissent was significant, why the concurrence is important and the most important part is the opinion. The opinion is the ideology of a majority of the Supreme Court justices speaking for 13 judicial circuits in America. All of America.

The Supreme Court has been around since the year 1789. It was created to interpret the laws of Congress and to correct circuit splits. Circuit splits happen when one circuit says something about a specific law and then another circuit says something else. For instance, that anti-abortion law in Alabama. This is a question of women's rights, medical science, and more importantly freedom of religion. Alabama is in the Eleventh Circuit. The Eleventh Circuit consists of three states which are Florida, Georgia, and Alabama. These are considered Deep Red (conservative) or the Bible Belt which consists of hardline Christians that are against abortion. However, being in the 11th Circuit is tough because the laws are not liberal and the 11th Circuit Court of Appeals is in Atlanta which consists of 20 judges, in which the majority is conservative. However, the circuits are broken down like this: the First Circuit which is the Districts of Maine, Massachusetts, New Hampshire, Puerto Rico, and Rhode Island. The U.S. Court of Appeals for the First Circuit is located in Massachusetts. The Second Circuit is New York, Connecticut, and Vermont; The Second Circuit Court of Appeals is in New York, New York. The Third Circuit is Delaware, New Jersey, Pennsylvania, and the Virgin Islands. The Third Circuit Court of Appeals is in Philadelphia. The Fourth Circuit consists of West Virginia, Virginia, North Carolina, South Carolina, Maryland. Richmond, VA, is where the Court of Appeals is located. The Fifth Circuit is Texas, Louisiana and Mississippi and its Court of Appeals is in Louisiana. The Sixth Circuit is Ohio, Kentucky, Tennessee, and Michigan. Its Court of Appeals is in Cincinnati, Ohio. The Seventh Circuit is Wisconsin, Illinois and Indiana. Chicago is where the Court of Appeals is located. The Eighth Circuit has North Dakota, South Dakota, Nebraska, Missouri, Arkansas, Iowa, and Minnesota. The Court of Appeals is located in St. Louis, Missouri. The Ninth Circuit is Washington State, Montana, Idaho, Nevada, California, Oregon, Arizona, Alaska, Hawaii, Northern Mariana Islands, and Guam (the Ninth is the biggest circuit).

The Court of Appeals is in San Francisco. You have the D.C. and Federal Circuits. That is thirteen circuits in total. The D.C. Circuit is for federal claims, i.e. lawsuits (suite-archaic) where it involves multi-jurisdictions, and the Federal Circuit is similar but mostly veteran issues and military. Once you know the significance of the Federal Court System and what it consists of, it is difficult to be mad when someone is convicted because you see things from a different perspective. It is not as bad as you would think because it sheds light on what a lot of society would not understand.

II

The date to file the 28 U.S.C. § 2255 was looming. I was focusing on filling the 2255 using ineffective assistance of counsel as my evidence because I was given two plea agreements, one for 0-19 years. Then two weeks before I was going to get sentence, I was given a new plea agreement of 15 years. Then to add insult to injury at my first plea hearing, the judge specifically told me he could not give me no more than 10 years. The moment I was sentenced to 15 years felt so surreal. I could not even imagine that something so simple could take my life away for 15 years. For about a year after I was sentenced, I was upset at myself. I felt like I wasn't supposed to receive 15 years for a gun. I was constantly asking myself, "How is this possible?" It fueled a drive like no other. I was determined to find out how this happened. I started doing my research, I found out the Armed Career Criminal Act (ACCA) was drafted in 1984 during the lame duck session that year in Congress. A lame duck session is when congress is about to change in composition because it is an election year. I was 5 years old then. Yes, five (5) years old, I did not even know how to spell Comprehensive Crime Control Act. The Comprehensive Crime Control Act came before the ACCA and was abrogated with the passing of the ACCA. Laws are created to protect the interest of the public; they are not supposed to destroy that interest by separating families and by victimizing minorities. The ACCA destroys and separates families. I felt like I was targeted because I did not want to cooperate, because I was black, because I was an immigrant. So many different thoughts ran through my mind, then I came to the realization that I had to keep moving and put my feelings to the side. The bottom line was that

I had to get my 2255 done. I went to Stoney, I had to admit he knew the law, but not all the issues. It's like doing something for so long you get stuck on auto-pilot. I felt good but I had doubts because he kept telling me about my case. When it comes to the law, everyone in prison is living their case, believe it or not (Christians call it carrying your cross). What you do while in prison is relatively up to you. Some people gamble, some do drugs, some become homosexuals, there is nothing in prison that is new. It is like you are in a time machine where old things never lose value and things that are new seem like an anomaly. I chose to educate myself about why and how could this happen. I would spend my days in the Law Library, studying and reading about ineffective assistance of counsel. I learned that an attorney is supposed to be an advocate for the defendant, and an adversary to the opposing party. In Cronic v. United States 468 U.S. 466 (1984), the case broke down and defined deficient performance. Strickland v. Washington 466 U.S. 464 (1984) also provided more elaboration on deficient performance.

That spoke about the cause and prejudice and what constitutes ineffective assistance. As I read these cases, I started seeing these people had worse situations. For instance, Leroy Washington, he killed someone out of desperation and pled out to death. "Who does that?" or "Who would allow someone to do that?" I was saying, my situation was nothing like that. I started reading on lawyers and the cases they wrote. I started noticing that the cases that mostly won were from big organizations or big firms. I would wonder if I would ever get a lawyer from a firm.

III

I finally got my issues together. It was one issue (the reason because long and drawn-out motions always take long to get granted). Ineffective assistance of counsel for failure to advise me out of the plea. I asked around, it was like people told me to do my own motion because I would know what my case is about, I was scared otherwise. I could have done better.

I sent in my 2255 in December 2013. 6 months later I still hadn't received a response, only until later did I receive it after I wrote the courts and let them know that the Supreme Court was reviewing for certiorari a case called Johnson v. United States 579 U.S. --- (2014). In Johnson at the time, they were asking whether possession of a short-barreled shotgun could be used as an enhancement for the Armed Career Criminal Act. A question, in fact, that was very good if you asked me, the lawyer that argued it was Katherine Menendez, believe it or not I liked her because of some of the cases she had litigated. Believe it or not, when I began to read law, I was able to see and observe that someone has an effort and put thought into writing the briefs. She did just as Brenda Bryn put an effort and thought into my appeals court briefs. I just felt she was overwhelmed, that was one of the reasons I did not want to contact her about my Supreme Court case. She is an excellent attorney, I have a lot of love and respect for her to this day. I submitted the 2255, at the time there was a lot of talk about the president issuing pardons (that was when Barack Obama was president), sentencing reform bills, and bringing 65% instead of 85%, and parole back. I had no faith in either of those scenarios. Don't get me wrong, Barack Obama was the first black President and he created Obama

Care. The fact remains clear he left a lot of people hanging (I know that there is only so much a person can do). I just did not believe in handouts and to this day I don't. I am appreciative for the efforts he provided for American minorities and general public. I am not one to say that I am going to jump for joy because they are black. Unfortunately the fact remains clear that sometimes your own people burn you quicker than your worst enemy.

IV

The 2255 was in and it seemed like forever to get a response. I was in my second tour in the legal research class, I was also taking classes on public speaking and learning about criminal thinking patterns for the first time in my life. I learned that I was thought like a criminal my entire life. Once I opened my eyes and realized that I had to change my thoughts through a process called cognitive behavioral therapy, or CBT. My perception was messed up. That was when I started to dig deeper and ask myself, who am I? Where am I going? Where is my life headed! I would walk the track in the rec yard and ask myself that. Walking the track is what people do to clear their head here. I would go back and forth problem solving in my mind. I would always see the same people from the compound sitting in the same spot every day. Since asking myself questions, as I said before. I started reading about history. I read Huey P. Newton's *Seize the Time* which is about the beginning of the Black Panther Party that opened my eyes even further about Co-intel Pro and the fact that they targeted blacks and they focused on keeping minorities divided and against each other. There were times I would pray to change that. The first step to change anything is awareness! Once you have awareness, then you can follow your own path towards change. I started to communicate more with Stone and other people that do law. I would share my viewpoints but I learned that when you do time, or been locked down for a while, you develop a pattern or a way of doing things that don't change. I was just coming in with only 4 years' time done. It was hard to adjust. I found it hard to adjust because I felt deep down that I was not going to do the time. I always believed in giving people the benefit of the doubt, little did I know that I was going to get a rude awakening.

V

In my third tour in legal research I was ready to teach because by then I figured out about clerks, judges, the rules and what it takes to write briefs, which is called the A, B, C of legal brief writing which is accurate, brief and concise. I knew how to write but remember what I said before about self-confidence: "Lack of self-confidence is worse than giving up." I was waiting for my final reply. I felt my 2255 could have been better, though Stone kept saying, "Don't let no one see your work, they're going to steal it." After reading *Seize the Time*, *Soul on Ice* and other books that clarify what blacks are going through in society this book was well written, what I learned from reading it was profound. It talked about minorities who are suppressed from growth by other minorities unfortunately, the struggles they faced and where if I am not mistaken, Huey called them Agent Provocateur, people the government uses to separate and cause confusion. Don't get me wrong, I give respect where it is due but some things are unnecessary. Also it is very transparent how these things happen you have to have an understanding about the system that was in place it was not a good system because once you are oppressed sometimes it is difficult to be awaken when the individuals that are to bring insight are the same ones working with the oppressors to bring you into a deeper pit of oppression.

VI

After I was able to file the response to my 2255, it was already about December 2014. At the end of December, I had gotten the final response from the report and recommendation (R & R). Under 28 U.S.C. § 636, a magistrate judge cannot make final rulings on civil matters in 2255 proceedings. A magistrate judge is the one who makes what is called an R&R or Report and Recommendation. Only Report and Recommendations and a plaintiff have 14 days to file a response to the R & R. I filed my response (after asking for an extension), then my District Court Judge, about a month later, denied my 2255 on December 9, 2014. Two weeks after that I filed for what is called a COA, or certificate of appealability. By then the Supreme Court, in Johnson v. United States, was asking the question of if the residual clause is unconstitutionally vague after oral arguments. In my mind I was saying, "Of course it's unconstitutionally vague." I shrugged it off, then proceeded to write. I told Stone to put it in my COA, then we started to argue and he told me I was too aggressive and too smart for my own good.

VII

Obama was in full swing with the clemency now. I had seen people actually start working out, programming, and getting ready to go home. Me, I was reading everything that came out about the clemency and I felt it had too many flaws to be helpful: 1) It gave power to the people who prosecuted you, 2) The requirements were either damn near impossible or difficult, 3) They gave free money to any lawyer willing to say, "I care, let's get them home," 4) Most of the lawyers were overworked with little knowledge, 5) The Office of the Pardon Attorney lacked resources. So, when I'd seen it for what it was, I kept it moving. My belief is, don't tell me, "SHOW ME." You can talk till your face turns purple, I am going to look at things for what it is. Then you got to remember the people who kept stressing to Obama, "You're the first black president, you got to do more." I shook my head, I prayed he'd leave a lasting legacy. My prayer was answered. During the clemency hype there was one particular counselor I have to give respect to: the counselor(s). They took care of many people's paperwork, who went home on clemency. She helped a lot of people go home. She actually gave me hope that people actually cared about people who had done wrong and <u>did their time</u>, so it was time for them to go home.

VIII

After the Supreme Court asked about the residual clause of the ACCA, everyone was scrambling to put the question in their motion. Remember, this was in 2015 and Public Defenders were "forbidden" to help inmates with 2255. I was blessed to get insight from Peter Birch. He gave me advice from time to time. On June 9, 2015, my request for COA (certificate of appealability) was denied. I was upset again because here I go getting denied again. But something inside me said, "Don't give up." In the beginning I felt the issue used in my 2255 was correct, but they cited in their denial cases that were irrelevant to my issue. I believed that the standards for COA were wrong and it was misplaced. Two weeks later they ruled on Johnson v. United States 135 S.Ct. 2251 (June 25, 2015). I read Johnson, that was kind of a terrible case. I later found out "the Supreme Court is the Court of Last Review, not First Review" (Id).

IX

I filed a Motion for Reconsideration. Stone and I kept bumping heads more and more. He finally told me it's best I file my own motions because I know too much! When I filed the Motion for Reconsideration, it was returned un-filed because I did not send it on time. So then the next step was the certiorari. When I needed the certiorari filed again, I went to Stone. He told me <u>not</u> to give up. Then by that time, Unique came from the Penn. Unique was like a big brother, he navigated me through the unnecessary nonsense. He was like a mentor to me as I was going through it with Stone. He told me to stop re-lying on people. I am too smart not to be believing in myself. Stone did the certiorari, I read it and became upset, my cellie at the time was like a little brother to me, so he asked what's wrong and I told him. Then he said, "Forget that, file your own motion, you smarter than that!"

X

I showed it to Unique and he was upset. We were sitting under the tree in the rec yard talking about the usual money we put away from industry checks, who I am talking to, just some small talk. By then, I was working in the prison commissary, so I was making good money. Unique said to throw out the motion, rewrite it, and as a man give him (Stone) props for teaching you, because that's what responsible men do. Just as it was said, it was done. I sent the motion off two weeks before it expired. I got an older Jamaican named Specie to type it (I did not know how to format nor edit motions at the time). He edited it for me and helped me format it, then me and him prayed over the motion so we would win and obtain victory. I went to church and asked that I obtain relief for the entire nation and people that needed to go home. At that time there was nothing coming out of the Eleventh Circuit. They created the circuit split with a case called In re Rivero 797 F.3d 986 (11th Cir. 2015) with the Seventh Circuit ruling opposite in Price v. United States 795 F.3d 731 (7th Cir. 2015). So I made that the point of my argument, I showed the circuit split that it was a case of significance and why the courts should accept it. I was nervous when I sent it because it was my first time going to the Supreme Court by myself. I called Peter to ask him what he thought, and I told him I was going to write Brenda Bryn to see what she could do. He told me that they were just talking about me and trying to see what they could do. I wrote her and she told Peter I should not write to her. I was glad I sent my motion off. Now I felt good about it. 1 knew I was eligible for relief, I just did not know when or where. But I knew it was coming! I did not know when but I knew it was coming.

XI

By this time I lost my job in commissary and I was doing law full time. Small things such as BP-8's. A BP-8 is the first step in the Administrative Remedy Program. Once you file that, it's more or less a notification that an error occurred and you want it resolved. If that is not resolved then you file a BP-9 to the warden, then a BP-10 to the Region. And then you file a BP-11 to Washington, D.C. Then you file a 2241 to the district court. Once you get to the district court, that's when they review all of the facts of the issue. I normally get those granted because I follow all the procedures.

XII

My Motion in the Supreme Court was sent back with a notice because I did not affix the Report & Recommendation from the magistrate judge. My case manager at the time said, "Well, well, looks like you got some work to do." She was fine, but she always talked smack like a true New Yorker. When I tried to put in a clemency, she said, "No. That's not 'you,' these forms are for people who don't know how to fight in court. That's not you. Figure it out!" That hit me like a dagger to the heart, but it made me stronger. That is exactly what I did. Just like anything I felt was done to make me feel bad.

XIII

After the certiorari was sent back, this time I was approached by the chief psychologist in the compound about joining the Skills Program. This time I was a Suicide Companion. A year into my time with the Suicide Watch Program, one of my friends killed himself. He laid on the train tracks. I was lost because he seemed normal. Joining the program meant something and it was a way to learn more about suicide and what causes it. I have gone to psychology. The skills program is an excellent program if you really want to do your time like that. I told psychology, "No, because I am not ready for that (being a mentor is not an easy task)." Plus, I told her I am focusing on my case and trying to help my cellie, who at the time had mental issues. She looked at who my cellie was and said to give it a try. I do not know what made me think it through, but I gave being a mentor a try. I went to her office and we spoke briefly about how I felt about it. And she told me to make my own decision and think it through. She asked me about my case. I told her what I was going through and she said, "Don't give up, Welch. Forget what they think, forget what they feel." So I took what she said. I took it to heart. This time I went and spoke to the doctor in A-1. We went back and forth. I told her I am rough around the edges. She said she knew all about me and it was nothing she was not used to. I asked about the program and how would I adjust. She told me that I would be given a grace period where I would have no cellie. I told her alright, I would give it a try. I gave her my word and I would do my best while there.

XIV

Everything from that point on is confidential with that program. I will not disclose anything further out of respect for the individual staff and inmates.

THE PHONE CALL THAT CHANGED MY LIFE

It was a hot September day in Central Florida. I just moved into the Skills Program, but my Unit Team was still in B-Unit. My counselor kept paging me for about a week. This time when he finally got in contact with me, he said, "Damn, if you that busy here, I could imagine you on the streets." I said, "Imagine that." I asked him, "What is it?" (He was upset because I wrote him up about not paying for being a wheelchair pusher.) He said, "Now some guy keeps calling here for you named Ali." I said, "Ali? Who is that?" He said, "I don't know, let's call him and see what he got to say." We called then he said, "Hello." I said, "What's up?" He said, "My name is Amir Ali. I am an associate attorney at Jenner & Block." I said, "<u>Who</u>?" Mr. Ali said, "Mr. Welch, right?" I said, "Yes!" Then Mr. Ali said, "I've been watching your case." I asked him, "How do I know you've been watching?" I asked him, "Have you been reading my handwritten motions?" Mr. Ali said, "Yes." He then said, "We are in a dilemma." I said, "<u>WE</u>. Who is we?" Mr. Ali said, "The partners of the firm." I said, "What's the dilemma?" Mr. Ali said, "See, we been following your case and the justices said we cannot review your case anymore unless we are assigned counsel." I said, "Assigned counsel, what do you mean assigned counsel? What's the <u>catch</u>?" Mr. Ali said, "We will represent you free of charge and we keep the petition that was filed the way it was filed." Mr. Ali said, "You get a Johnson case, right?" I said, "Yeah, I do have a Johnson case." I told him, "Johnson is retroactive." Mr. Ali said, "Not in the Eleventh Circuit." I said, "I know, it is because of In re: Rivero." In re: Rivero was decided right before my 2R U.S.C. § 2255 was pending so it barred a lot of people from getting the retroactivity of Johnson v. United States. At the time the Eleventh Circuit was difficult because of the case laws that were in place. We talked for an hour, about what he had been studying, then Mr. Ali said he was going to send me an engagement letter in the mail, he also wanted to give me his email so that I could stay in contact with him, and he was going to send me an agreement in the email. I said, "Alright." The counselor said, "Finally you got to make your call." I said, "Yep! Sounds like it is going to be one of many to come." Which it was! Mr. Ali accepted the email request. I told him, "Thank you! For wanting to represent me. I appreciate the fact that you are taking the time to represent me." Then he sent me a reply with the engagement letter. In the engagement letter, it explained the terms of the agreement then asked for my digital signature. I sent it. After that, the rest is history.

XV

Over the course of the next couple months I finally felt like someone was listening to me. I started reading newsletters about cases pending review in the Supreme Court. One of the main things I always did that no one really knew was that I was a regular subscriber to legal newsletters. In fact, prior to filing my § 2255, I was emailing Jeremy Gordon, Jose Francisco, Brandon Sample, LISA, Craig Coscerelli, George Carlton, and Martha Shein in Atlanta, among others. I had asked Jeremy Gordon, and Jose Francisco, to help me file certiorari. Everyone told me that I got it, just "do you." So I did me. Once I got with Jenner & Block, I have to admit, it changed my perspective about attorneys. On the second phone call with Amir I asked him who he had represented. Amir said, "I just won a case called Brumfield v. Cain," and he told me he is going to send me a bio of attorneys on my case then I said okay.

XVI

We started talking about stare decisis, and retroactivity and he asked me who filed the petition. I told him I did. Then I asked him what was going on with me. Amir said he was going to stay on board and that he was going to have a meeting with the Department of Justice about my case and I said, "Why would you have a meeting about me?" He said it is standard procedure. Then he would ask why am I fighting so hard and I told him that I am a single father, my mother has my kids, and it eats me up inside that I am not there for them. He said he understood. I told him, "This is my life. When the phone hangs up, you go home with your wife, I go to a unit or a cell with the possibility that I might get into a fight or someone might feel threatened or intimidated or might want to retaliate for something that happened in the past." He said okay. We ended that call.

XVII

Amir called back about a week later, he told me that he got the letter I wrote. It was an introductory letter telling him who I was, where I was from, and what I was doing. He said he was impressed and that guys in my situation normally give up or just don't care anymore. I told him my kids are at that age and they need me. He then told me that the meeting with the Department of Justice went well. By this point it was October 2015, it seemed as if everything was happening fast. I kept asking, "Since when does the Department of Justice care about its inmates?" Amir told me, "The courts have gone on recess until January. When they come back they're going to rule on if I get granted cert review." By then people started telling me that I was not going to get it. I was only going to get G.V.R. G.V.R. means "grant, vacate, and remand," meaning they were going to send it back to the lower courts. I was watching the courts, I noticed that everyone was filing second and successive which is based on 28 U.S.C. § 2244. I was laughing to myself because I was thinking about the judges that were reading and laughing to themselves. Also you can't appeal second and successive application to the Supreme Court. The A.E.D.P.A. Bill stated that you cannot file an appeal on an application under 28 U.S.C. § 2244 a.k.a. Second and Successive when the denial list was coming out and all you were seek was writ of certiorari denied for

In re: Williams

In re: Johnson

In re: Walter

It was like a couple hundred or so cases that were denied. By then the Supreme Courts started shifting and granting applications in light of Johnson v. U.S. 135 S.Ct. 2551 (2015). I started watching the liberal courts like the Second Circuit. They granted an application in Freeman v. United States (2d Cir. 2016), which was granted a stay that was a murder case and in California they had a case called United States v. Luong (9th Cir.). From the Ninth Circuit, it was put on stay pending the review in Welch. Then in the Fourth Circuit they had United States v. Edmondson (4th Cir.).

The Fourth Circuit was not liberal at all. In fact, they are Hardline Bible Belt. Let's just keep it real for one moment, any state that has been known for slavery, cotton, and tobacco, it is not rocket science what the state's constitution would be based on or how they feel about the Thirteenth Amendment of the U.S. Constitution. Please know and believe, just because slavery is abolished, understand what moral servitude is, notice it is does not say, "They shall not obtain a conviction for moral servitude through trickery based on race, gender, or social class." Now when that happens, we will have a deep conversation on justice as for anything else, I will be sitting back enjoying the view of what's to come. What was to come actually came after the U.S. elections in 2016. America took a turn for the worst but remember it has to get worst in order for things to become better.

XVIII

The date was January 8, 2016. The Supreme Court had a conference on the 7th and they were going to make announcements on Friday for cases granted. Conference is when the court has a private meeting on cases to be heard. No one knows beforehand which cases will be heard. I am grateful for the Honorable Justices who answered my prayers to solve the issues. The eventual argument at the Eleventh Circuit Court of Appeals was whether to label it as nonviolent robbery. Due to the reason given in Welch case, it helped a lot of people in deciding that the decision in Johnson was to be retroactive which clarified the elements clause of the ACCA. The courts have been arguing about the application of the different sections of the ACCA for years. For instance, James v. United States 553 U.S. 192 (2008), Begay v. United States 553 U.S. 137 (2008), Sykes v. United States 131 S.Ct. 2267 (2011), and Chambers v. United States 555 U.S. 122 (2009) Id. These cases touched upon the ACCA in some form or another, it was a problem with the courts because of the interpretation and since the ACCA was enacted there have been numerous ambiguities, so Johnson v. United States 135 S.Ct. 2251 (2015) was a big step in the right direction.

When certiorari was granted, I not only started reading more newsletters, I started reading a site called Scotus blog. Scotus stands for Supreme Court of the United States. One person I have a lot of respect for is Professor Rory Little. He wrote an interesting article about my case in which he spoke about Johnson being retroactive and how I wrote the motion very "scant" and that this has not happened since Clarence Earl Gideon from Gideon v. Wainwright

373 U.S. 335 (1963). At times it was frustrating but believe it or not, my attorneys prepared me for it. They continuously called me and instructed me about press releases, and how to avoid the media. I have to say that being an avid reader did not help the situation at all. I read the Criminal Law Reporter every week religiously. What I also learned from my attorneys at Jenner & Block was that high-profile cases get assigned reporters for the Criminal Law Reporter. It was Jessica DaSilva and Kimberly Strawbridge Robinson. They wrote the first article I read after I won certiorari review. They wrote that I "bucked" the Supreme Court trend that I did not get a re-list and the Supreme Court had only done that four times that term, and it is a notable decision to watch; I spent a lot of time in the Law Library researching my issue. My attorneys were Lindsay Harrison, Amir Ali, Jessica Ring-Amunson, Ishan Bhabha, Joshua Parker, Mathew Price, David Debruin. R. Trent McCotter, Paul M. Smith, Adam G. Uniknowsky, and Benjamin M. Eidelson (James Dawson came on board in November 2016). I am thankful for the attorneys, I was blessed to have them on my team. I am thankful for the National Association of Criminal Defense Lawyers (NACDL). I am also thankful for the Federal Public Defenders Office(s) all over America, Brenda Bryn, Peter Birch, Michael Caruso, Conrad Kahn, Alison Guilardo, Janice Berman, Rosemary Cakmis, and all Public Defenders who prayed for my victory and attorneys who understood my drive and what my true motivations are.

XVIX

The number one in my life are my children. Even though I am strict with them, there is not a day that goes by where I do not think about them.

With the news articles, it was as if people were writing about my case every week. Some good, some bad. I did not like when they were talking about my attorneys at that time. Amir was my point of contact at Jenner & Block. After the articles were out, that was when everything on the compound went from bad to worse. People that were doing law for years started saying I stole their idea, that I don't know what I was doing, and "them lawyers going to turn their backs on me." You name it. I heard it. And it hurt more hearing it from Stone. I had a lot of respect for him. I even told him, "Thank you for teaching me." He told me that I changed what he did and

"that's all you." I thought that was an honorable thing for him to say that. Unique told me not to sweat it and called me "Fredrick Douglass and the Supreme Court Gangster."

The younger guys on the compound called me SCG, short for "Supreme Court Gangster." Unique said gangsters come in all shapes, sizes, and colors. He gave me a dap (otherwise known as a fist bump) and a hug and said, "I am proud of you and always remember, it's lonely at the top but it's a hell of a view." My view on the law changed after that because I began to realize that "facts" are what can free you or hold you! The U.S. Constitution works on both sides, once you apply it correctly.

I started to see the pain of people suffering. One thing about me is when I talk to you, I have to look into your eyes. If your eyes shift, I lose interest in your conversation. I started talking to people more. I was in the Skills Program, so I learned about criminal behavior and criminal thinking and the difference between lifestyle criminals. When I started learning about lifestyle criminals it gave me a different outlook on life and people with mental issues. When I started talking to people about their case I would pay attention to their "vibe" or energy. It is weird, I could always read people. A lot of people on the compound were stuck, as to what's next with the "WELCH Doctrine" and how it was going to apply. I started getting second and successive forms and helping people fill them out. At this time, "Jail House Lawyers" were charging people anywhere from $500 to $1,000. Yep, believe it or not, I read Avery v. Johnson and yes, if it is necessary, you charge. But not the person who literally has nothing in their locker and who barely makes enough for soup every month, where their "entire" family had written them off.

XX

I had gotten what was called an expedited briefing schedule (Feb. 2016). So that means my briefs and moot hearing, and order of attorneys had to be in on an expedited schedule. Our first brief was due in February with oral argument due March 30, 2016. Before we filed, Amir called me and told me that the solicitor general changed position and conceded that Johnson was "retroactive." He said he was shocked because it was a good thing. I said, "Of course, they are going to concede." They recommended a G.V.R. then right after that, they granted Montgomery v. Louisiana 136 S.Ct. 718 (2016) and ruled Miller v. Alabama, retroactive, that was a blessing from above because that was a sign that they were going to rule in my favor. Then shortly after Justice Antonin Gregory Scalia passed away. I said, "God! Why now, may his soul rest in peace." I was sad to hear that news. I called Amir and told him. He said, "What? I had seen it on FOX News." In all actuality, my heart sank because I knew his ideology on law, his explanations as a constitutionalist, that's how I get it. I was thinking that when Justice Scalia would read it he would say to Justice C. Thomas, "Hey! Clarence, the kid is right. He finally got it. Someone finally got it!" I thought about the Senate and the fight they were giving Obama and the next pick he was going to pick Sri Srinivasan or Judge Merrick Garland. I was aware of Merrick Garland because a lot of my attorneys at Jenner & Block clerked for him and knew him directly.

XXI

When you say I felt like the people lost a good man, that hurt because I had a lot of respect for Justice Scalia. I was not only saddened by the loss I felt overwhelmed. I started to wonder who was going to have the same reasoning with the issue I raised? Was it going according to the way I wrote the petition? One thing about being an analytical thinker is that it is a gift and a curse. I have great respect for all the Honorable Judges who reach the level of being a Supreme Court Justice. It carries a lot or responsibility about issues that are of significance to American jurisprudence.

That month was rough for me. I had gone from 9 justices down to 8 and it looked as if there was not going to be another justice for the hearing. I was walking in the rec yard and Unique was walking with someone. They were arguing, so I walked the other way to avoid getting into it. Then the person started getting in my face, so I started punching him in the face. I backed up and told him, "Alright, let's take it to the bathroom." Then a crowd starting gathering, they said, "Oh, sh—" Welch fighting. I followed him to the bathroom, he picked up a mop stick and it broke over my head. I was still standing. I wanted to kill him because I felt he was a coward for grabbing a weapon. I was taken to the S.H.U. because I had a lump on my head and the stick was broken. This was when things started getting strange when I went to the Special Housing Unit, otherwise known as the S.H.U. "Special Housing Unit" S.I.S. pulled me out of the cell. Before they pulled me out, I was in the cell with someone named Cuz. Everything he said ended with "Cuz, Cuz." The officer said, "Welch, I am going to find you a good cellie" (in the S.H.U. your cellie makes time easier). When the officer said, "Welch, I got you a good cel-lie," Cuz went leftfield and said, "Which Welch? Are you the Welch from the Welch case?" Then I said, "Gregory Welch v. United States 15-6418, writ of certiorari granted January 8, 2016." He said, "Your name is on my paperwork, Cuz." Then he got on the vent (in prison, the vent is like a phone), then he said, "Pac-Man, I got Welch in my cell," then he said, "Welch. Yeah, Supreme Court Welch." Then Pac-man said, "Tell Welch I want to holla at him then." The officer came and said, "Welch, phone call." Then they took me to a room for an interview. I was still dazed, I remember he said, "I don't know who you are but when lawyers and private investigators call asking questions about why you in the S.H.U. that means something." Then he said he spoke to my attor-ney and my mother. Then he asked, "Do you have any problems with the per-son who hit you?" Then I said, "I do not remember." Then I went to my cell, then I was escorted back, the S.H.U. was a prison within the prison. Believe it or not, almost everyone in prison takes a trip there whether for investigation or having a run-in with the wrong officer, Lt. or any staff member that could have a bad day. Sometimes that is the consequence you have to pay. I was out after about a week. They asked if me and the person were alright. I said, "I am cool." They told me if he got transferred and got killed in another spot, they were going to charge me with murder. In the back of my mind, I was laughing. Prior to coming out, Amir came and saw me while in the S.H.U. I had a full beard when I had seen him. I salaam him and gave him a hug. He asked me if I was alright. I said, "No. I need some water." I told him I was up all night breaking down the habeas corpus to my cellie and other people on the tier.

It was pretty noisy at night because you might have some people who would sleep all day and would stay up all night. I am no different. He told me I was going to be alright. He asked me if I did law. I told him, "Yeah." How could he tell? I told him I was from Kingston, Jamaica, I migrated to Brooklyn, then we were separated from our mother and placed in an orphanage. Then when we came out the orphanage, we moved back with our mother. Then we moved to Florida. I started robbing when I was young. He looked at me sur-prised, then we spoke about the law and asked him, "How did you find me?" He told me that he had been watching the docket. Then I said, "You were am-bulance chasing." In the legal world, ambulance chasers are lawyers who follow cases, hoping to get picked up by the client, then he tried to pass it off to Trent.

I said, "Hell naw. He should be the one getting the props for finding me." I told him that he got a good vibe and he said they're going to fight to get me out and I asked, "How many people are going to be affected?" And he said, "Right now, it is about 10,000 to 15,000." He said, "If the opinion goes right, it can help about 20,000 instantly." I said, "How do you know that?" He said, "It is called a statistical analysis." I said, "They crunch the numbers." He said, "Yep." So I said, "Who is the mastermind behind this?" We were eating, I almost choked when he said that. I said, "Damn, they really do respect gangster." I mean, I read some cases in the Supreme Court that were messed up. For instance, Scott v. <u>Negro</u> London, where you were considered to be someone's property. The Dred Scott case, where you were considered less than human. Plessy v. Ferguson, where if you had one drop of Negro blood, you were a "nigger." Yeah, they were racist. I learned that history is what makes the world the way it is. I can either learn from it and prosper or become upset.

XXII

Here I am communicating with one of the top appellate attorneys in D.C. about getting out of prison. "Who does that?" He said he had to leave, then he asked the C.O. to give me my legal work. Then he said, "No." I told him the officer likes to harass.

Then he told me to pick and choose my battles wisely. I told him right is right and wrong is wrong. While we were on visit, people were pointing at me and Amir. I did not know why, because I was still feeling distracted, I had a big lump on my head. It went down but I still felt queasy when I stood up sometimes and when I laid down I would fall asleep. He gave me a hug good-bye and told me to take care. Then I was handcuffed and taken back to be strip-searched and taken back to the cell. The officer said, "So you're the famous Supreme Court Welch." I said, "Who, me? Naw, never, that I don't nothing about no law, wrong guy." Then he said, "Why your lawyer came and see you when you're locked up? And he is no bullshit one either. He is a good lawyer." I said, "To keep tabs on me. I guess, I don't know." He said, "One thing about you, Welch, you love playing like you stupid." I said, "Why not? Everybody likes to have fun from time to time." Then he said, "Alright." I made it to my cell. Cuz said, "some people came to see you." I said, "what people? Why you in my business?" He said, "They fuck with you, don't they?" I said, "Naw, homie, you asking too many questions." Two days after that I was taken out the S.H.U. It was called a S.H.U. Kickout. A S.H.U. Kickout was when they let people out back on the compound. I went back to the Skills Program. I felt bad, embarrassed, like I let my participant down. He kept my bedspread, my property in my locker. It was like I never went anywhere. I gave him a hug and said, "What up, homie?" He said, "You alright?" I said, "I am good." He said, "I heard what happened." He said, "It got the best of you." He was talking about my temper. We prayed. Then he told me to think about the people who cared about me. I said alright. I laid down. I saw Unique, he gave me a hug, then he said that I was not wrong for fighting and that his homeboy was a coward for picking up a weapon. That was not a fair fight. I said now, "I am good," I thought to myself how many people play up on me and then have hate in their heart. I proceeded to stay to myself again. The date for my certiorari was getting close. I got out of the S.H.U. on March 6. I got a legal call to authorize a moot hearing for someone from Jones Day to be on the panel of the moot hearing. A moot hearing is a practice hearing for the attorneys to learn their strengths and weaknesses and to be prepared for the judges. I would say Amir is a hard worker and the senior partners at Jenner would go hard, they earned my respect. Amir would email me periodically to keep me posted about what's going on. I was thinking how would this work out with 8 justices. I prayed constantly. I fasted on March 30, 2016. I also prayed. People were coming up to me saying today was the day. Welch, I heard about so many blogs. I read so many. I was getting frustrated but I always felt that it was going to be alright. After the argument Amir and about five attorneys from Jenner called, they said the argument went great. I asked, "What are the odds?" Josh yelled out, "70% Greg guaranteed." Lyndsay said, "Amir did an excellent job." Then comes the stress. "When was the ruling going to be published?" I was saying that it could not be in June because Johnson was to expire in June. So how would that work out? I read the blogs; they said the argument went well/ Everyone was saying I was going to lose because it's only 8 justices. But I was thinking, "Man, how is this going to work out?" One week went by. Nothing. Then on Monday, April 18, 2016, my email was going crazy. The email system in the Federal Bureau of Prisons is corrlincs. Corrlincs is how we would get emails; we get to use 30 contacts and they can send as many emails as possible. When Welch v. United States was granted every criminal defense lawyer and appeals attorney was excited because they had a client that had a Johnson retroactivity issue.

XXIII

Prior to winning, the 11th Circuit started staying cases in abeyance, pending the decision in Welch. I filed about 10 seconds and successive to the 11th Circuit. They denied a case called in re: Robinson (2016) and they used the opinion to list the cases that need to be filed in another petition. The court was flooded with Johnson and Welch petitions. It was crazy because I did not know that there were so many ACCA cases. The courts started to extend Johnson to the 924(c) in my brief from the Supreme Court. The government stated that "any statute that had the residual clause language would be void for vagueness brief for the government page 54," and they also briefed that in another case called Dimaya v. Lynch 803 F.3d 1110 (2015). Dimaya also went on and extended Johnson to the residual clause of the 16(b). That case was also retroactive. It extended to another case called United States v. Davis, Davis extended Johnson to the 924c and made the residual clause unconstitutional.

XXIV

When I won, it was like my life changed. Everyone was basically running around. I heard people getting called to R&D every five minutes. "Anthony Johnson. Report to R&D." R&D stands for Receiving and Discharge. Anthony Johnson was from In re: Johnson (2016). Then at about 4 o'clock count the next day, people getting shuffled off the compound every second[1]. "Aye, you got to go, time to leave."

People were coming up to me, "Aye, Welch, man, so and so charging me 500. I don't got it. Help me out." "I got you." I hate being lied to so I said, "Better yet, I am going to give you a number. Call them and tell them Welch gave you the number." He called and then he came to me and said, "She said to tell you 'thank you' and she had my case on her desk." The most notable was an O.G. original gangster from Miami stepping up to me and said, "Say, Youngblood, you Welch, right?" I said, "Yeah." He shook my hand and said, "Thank you." Then he said, "Welch, f*** them niggas, I been down 20 years and I never seen a black man beat them, I respect you, Welch." Later that day I would pray and thank God. He asked me, "What do I do?" I told him, "I got you." He said he had a Mathis v. United States issue. So I broke down Mathis and how it would apply. Then he said, "Are you a computer?" I said, "Nah, I have a photographic memory." He said, "You are blessed and God is going to continue blessing you." Every time he saw me, he said, "What's up?" Then one day he said, "Welch, I missed my kids growing up." Man, that was when

---

[1] It felt really good seeing people going home because it seemed as if you can see the look of happiness on their faces like they are relieved and they have no stress.

I realized it was not about me. I realized there were people that have been dead that needed resurrection and that it was bigger than me that moment I started to understand that the system was destroying lives that moment gave me a sense of awareness of what part I played.

XXV

O.G. came back to me and told me that his lawyer was full of it and he was tired of the back-and-forth with them. I said, "Nah, you got to give them people a chance cause they are probably busy and they have a lot going on." He said, "From you, Welch, I will hear them out." Then I told him that Mathis v. United States applied to his burglary offense and that they were waiting on the ruling which was due in June. I would go to the rec yard by the baseball field and just clear my head. Process my thoughts. Think about "what next." So what happened next was, someone came to me and said, "You Welch, right?" I said, "Yeah, what's up?" He said that I helped his buddy get 15 years off his sentence and he wanted me to help him and he had a life sentence. I told him, "Nonsense, who really gets life for a gun?" Then he explained to me that he beat the death penalty in the state, so when he beat death row, the U.S. Marshalls were waiting for him with a federal indictment. If you do not know, the U.S. Marshalls Service is a fugitive transport service for the federal government. They issue warrants, execute apprehension of fugitives and assets worldwide on behalf of the federal government. Now what a lot of people do not know is once they issue an indictment, they can get you any time after the indictment is issued (before the statute of limitation runs out). Murder is the one of the main statutes that carry no statute of limitation. Literally "any time." So I told him, "They pulled the 'oke doke' on you, huh?" He said, "Welch, I need you." I said, "I got you. Where are you from in Florida?" He said his case was out of Central Florida. I said, "This is what you do. I am going to give you the number to the Federal Public Defender in Orlando." Obama just issued an omnibus executive order to the Federal Defenders and eligible CJA attorneys. CJA stands for the Criminal Justice Act, and this was drafted for indigent defendants to receive reasonable attorneys without paying any fees. The attorneys, in turn, would get a government voucher for representation, and for transcripts, investigations, documents and expert witnesses involved with the case. An omnibus bill is an equitable pleading by which a claimant brings a claim in a court of equity. Before the merger of law and equity, the bill in equity was analogous to a declamation in law. The declaration in law was that Johnson was deemed retroactive and that you are not in prison legally any more. "A rule is substantive rather than procedural when it alters the range of conduct or the class of persons convicted" (Welch v. United States 136 S.Ct. 1257, 1265 (2016) quoting Schriro v. Summerlin 542 U.S. 348 (2004)). He caught up to me about a month or two later. I was, as usual, sitting on the bench and this time he was playing baseball. I was being sarcastic and cracking jokes. He gave me the most vicious look. He hit the ball, then I followed him to first base and said, "That was not 'Nothing.'" Then he said, "Welch, guess what?" I said, "What?" "You suck at baseball." "Screw you, dude." I laughed and said, "What's up, homie?" He said, "The lawyer said I was eligible for time served." I said, "No shit. That's a blessing. Thank God. I told you it was going to be over soon." I felt good from that because I understood where he was coming from and I understood his pain. It felt as if I was being used as a vessel by God to help people. But truthfully, I am selfish. I am a textbook definition of it. So I knew it had to be a higher power and nothing short of it.

XXIV

The day was May 20, 2016. I received a letter in the mail that the Eleventh Circuit granted my certificate of appealability. I felt good because now I could have a fair fight with them because when they had denied my motion the first time, that hurt. Then a couple days later, I received another letter that they denied my second recall mandate. A recall mandate is under Federal Rules of Appellate Procedure 41. That is filed asking the Court to recall the mandate or stay the mandate. It can be filed any time but there is a trick to it. You have to send a copy to the Solicitor General Office, <u>not</u> the A.U.S.A. of the circuit you are from because you are going to get denied for certain if you do that. The solicitor general review appeal cases for en banc review certiorari, habeas corpus, mandamus, and cases of national importance. When I filed my § 2255, it was an original 2255, the 2255 that was drafted in 1948 by Congress. It is called an A0243 form meaning administrative order[2] form 243. The 2255 was a short stop from the 2241, the 28 U.S.C. § 2241 title is AO 242[3]. These forms can only work for you, when and if you use them to state the right claim and exercise due diligence with accuracy and clarity. Angry litigation is only to get you more upset, frustrated, and sent to an unpleasant part of the prison (trust me, the S.H.U. is nothing nice). The writ of habeas corpus was created in 1779 based on the All Writs Act. It is covered under 28 U.S.C. § 1651. Title 28 is for the judiciary meaning judges. The <u>habeas corpus</u> was created to <u>free</u> slaves and or property that was taken and the word "habeas" means "bring," "corpus"

---

[2] Administrative order means it came from a administrative agency.
[3] The numbers are listed in the top left corner if the forms.

the "body," or "deliver the body to its owner." It is sad, but true. It was based on capturing freed slaves and returning them back to their owner. It is a significant part of history that cannot be erased or forgotten. That is another reason for me to fight. Sometimes I would read over my briefs and some of the cases I would read were from the Antebellum era. The Antebellum era was pre-Civil War, around 1847. Those were good cases (even though they were not cited, the cases used were progeny[4] cases from them, for instance, ex-parte Siebold that clarified retroactivity since 1880). Another antebellum case was Dred Scott v. Sanford or the Dred Scott case. I loved that case because I looked him up and his Supreme Court picture where he looked pissed off like he was saying, "How could they say I am not 100% human?" That is another part of history which I love and appreciate even more. Once the C.O.A. was granted, I felt very good. Things started looking up for me.

---

[4] Progeny (n) means offspring.

XXV

Then I got assigned A.U.S.A. Gwendolyn Stamper. Man, she was tough. She was an Obama appointee, I have to admit she was going hard. We filed our first brief in June 2016, then the Pulse shootings happened. That hurt because I knew some women who were there that night, they were not hurt, they told me about the chaos and smelling death. That was sad. I believe people should not suffer because of someone else's ignorance. That was a sad day in the world. Once we filed our first brief, the government had 30 days to respond. The government filed a motion for an extension of time. By that time Amir filed a motion to oppose that motion for extension of time. That pissed the government off because they were used to defendants laying down and not fighting. Amir called me prior to putting the first initial brief in. I have to say I was impressed with the way the brief was put together. They clarified the timeline of the robberies. We were stuck though because the Eleventh Circuit was set to argue a case called Seabrooks v. United States. He had similar priors but his were armed robberies. Armed robberies in Florida carry a higher penalty. The irony behind that is the statute 812.13 is indivisible, and Mathis v. United States, Descamps v. United States and Moncrieff v. Holder all clarify what's called the "least culpable conduct standard of an offense." Moncrieff clarified not only the least culpable conduct standard of an offense for drug convictions. The Florida Robbery is a statute with multiple meaning such as Florida Felony Drug Statute 893.13. Both statutes have been abrogated (abrogated means it was changed). The 812.13 was changed in 1999 and it included robbery by sudden snatching 812.13(1). That was what we were challenging. The timeframe, the intra circuit split, and the law of the case doctrine. First we are going to talk about the intra circuit split. The intra circuit split I am talking about is the 4th DCA in Florida (Fourth District Court of Appeals). The 4th DCA is comprised of Broward & Palm Beach counties, the 3rd DCA is Dade, Monroe, and Manatee counties. I am mentioning the counties where they are challenging the crime of violence in the robbery by sudden snatching. In Dade it could be done without but in Broward and Palm Beach they had no clear answer as to what the interpretation was. They had Robinson v. State, which was a state Supreme Court case and the case itself had no bearing on Florida robberies before 1997 and United States v. McNeil said that they got to use the interpretation of the law at the time when sentencing a defendant so I was caught in a catch-22. Then we had the law of the case doctrine[5], the law of the case doctrine is based on the law that was first created and that any future litigation is based by the first case unless that first case is overruled by the Supreme Court or an en banc[6] court and that is governed by Davis v. United States (1974). In our first brief, we made an excellent argument. Well, election time was rolling around and Trump was in full swing with the crooked Hillary statements and "lock her up." Believe it or not, politics affect Supreme Court cases because if your case falls in a particular category, it would call into question of how the justices feel or how they choose to interpret the issue. And you have to remember that Supreme Court is the "Court of Last Review" and "Not First View."

---

[5] Law of the case doctrine means a court will generally refuse to consider an issue that was previously raised in the same court higher court of a court in the same case.

[6] The en banc court is a court of judges who elect to re-hear a case with more judges.

XXV

They decided United States v. Seabrooks in the Eleventh Circuit Court of Appeals. He was denied but there was a good dissent that said Welch is still good law. Then they had another case that clarified the felony battery that was a favorable ruling. The government filed for a stay pending en banc review, we opposed the stay then we had to wait until a judge gave the order on if they were going to grant or deny the stay. They granted the government's request for stay pending the decision in Vail-Bailon (felony battery).

In that case they ruled in my favor, on one of the issues I was raising, which was, Florida felony battery is not a crime of violence. On that note I knew it was not good (me and the attorneys were just rolling the dice). When the court granted the government request, the counselor gave me the legal mail. It was counselor. After she gave me the mail she stated, "Who are you?" I asked, "Do I know you?" She stated, "I don't know, do you?" I signed for my legal mail, then left. The following couple days I was called back to her unit for a legal call. She was the best counselor at the time because she gave people what they had coming. This time she said, "You're Welch." Then I said, "Who, me? Naw, don't know that guy." She said, "You messing with me?" I said, "Maybe." Then her orderly walked in and said, "Welch," and I said, "Where he at?" Then the orderly said, "Stop playing." Said, "Alright, you got that, what's up?" She started saying, "You get me putting in overtime doing these legal calls, case managers, unit managers, counselors all over the B.O.P. putting in the immediate release paperwork for inmates all over and here you are blending in like your normal." I said, "Hold up, I am from the hood." She said, "I heard about you from one of my girlfriends. She is a public defender." I said, "What district?" She said, "The middle district." I said, "I bet I know her." She said, "I know, she told me to tell you 'hi' and she is praying for you." I said, "I could imagine." Then she was saying she was looking at my name on the fax for a legal call. I said, "Yep, that's me." By this time it was around September and everyone was anticipating Hillary to win. I was fighting against the A.E.D.P.A.[7] that Bill Clinton signed into law. I remember I took a sentence in 1995 to receive a lenient plea while I could so a majority of the public did not understand that type of evil. I would rather accept someone who tells you who they are than someone who is seasoned in manipulation. Trump was telling you who he is. I did my research on the Democratic Party and did not say "no" but "hell no." An organization is as good as its foundation and if the foundation was built on racism and hatred, I guess the rest is self-explanatory. Please don't think I support racism in any way, because I don't, but what goes on in the dark will come to light. Trump was supporting Bill and Hillary for years, then all of a sudden he runs for president. My ancestors would disown me if I supported any of that.

---

[7] ANTI and Effective Death Penalty Act 1996

XXVI

I finally got my legal call, then I asked Amir, "what is the plan that Jenner & Block has for me? I heard they wanted me to go to law school and take the option of being either a lawyer or a law clerk." He said, "One of those options is already in the works."

We spoke about the election, he asked me if I am asking people to vote for Hillary. I did not respond. I told him I read some of her and Bill Clinton's published emails before I came in and I know what they are about. I said I'd rather roll the dice than be burned again. He said, "Interesting." We started talking about different strategies he wanted to use to brief the argument before the Eleventh Circuit. He said that he was open for suggestions. The judge said that they wanted a stay because we were being too aggressive in opposing the government request for extension of time, I was getting frustrated with the process and people kept asking, "When you going home?" People were constantly going home and at this point it was a blessing experiencing that. Could you imagine someone telling you that you were going to get denied or going to get granted and they knew nothing about the sentencing guidelines nor do they know about what session they are in Congress, what a bill of attainder is, who the Speaker of the House is? Let them tell it, I was denied and my lawyer set me up.

I always politely dismiss any false claims, correct them, then continue moving forward. Besides that, I do not have time for that. I am always busy either with my kids, girlfriend(s), brothers, family or business ventures. I am really not the type to linger about prison politics. That is a waste of time and most of it is really tabloids so I keep it moving. As I waited for them to lift the stay, the election drew upon us. Man, that was a shot. The crazy part was that some of Trump's homeboys were in prison with me and they said, "Greg Welch." I said, "Yeah." And he said, "You going to be alright, buddy, just hang in there." I said to myself, "Why this got to happen to me?" Then I had went back to see the counselor. This time she said, "1) You are a black man in America with street smarts and book smarts, you are dangerous." I asked, "How do you know?" She told me, "Every week a different call comes in to talk to you or a call to ask about you or is filling something with your name on it." She said, "2) The Supreme Court of the United States know you. They study you, watch you. If you think them people going to let you get out and waste your life, you are not the person I know you are." Those statements hit me in the chest real hard. She said everything while looking in my eyes. I asked, "How do you know I am qualified to do that?" Then this is what happened: "The way you talk, the way people listen, it is with effortless ease." Coming from her meant a lot because she is from the streets as well. So I had a lot of respect for what she said. She knew who I was now and she figured I was not a creep. Going on with my situation, I have to give her maximum respect.

XXVI

After the election, all of America was in shock because they thought Hillary was going to win. I said, "Thank God." I already knew how people smile in your face and deep down it is not worth anything. I prayed Obama would stand firm on a lot of sentencing and good time credit issues, conspiracy-relevant conduct issues, but the bottom line, he gave up on men. "Men" in federal prison are people who never compromised their values. Responsible, straight-up honest people that do their time. I felt left out. That was another reason why I was determined to fight. Besides my kids, I felt I did less than keep moving forward. The only thing that upset me with the new administration was the fact Jeff Sessions was going to be the Attorney General. That was terrible at that time, and who would replace Justice Scalia? He was a great justice. Even under the Chief Justice Roberts, who is also a good justice. He has written many opinions, but I have read a few of them. Justices Sotomayor, Ginsberg, Kegan, and Breyer have been liberal in their views and on many topics were on point. Sometimes when I would read the opinions I would be stuck, but sometimes when I would look into the statutes and the circuit splits, it would give more clarity. For instance, Justice Alito would almost always dissent in criminal cases like in Curtis Johnson; he dissented in Samuel Johnson. Justice Kennedy (he wrote the opinion in Welch), he has been the swing vote. The swing vote is someone who clarifies the issue, the deciding factor, like a plurality opinion. It's like a 4-1-4 where there is one concurring opinion. Justice Sotomayor wrote one in Freeman v. United States, breaking down the context of the Rule 11(c) plea agreement. Plurality opinions are good but they leave a lot of "what-ifs," case in point majority opinions and per curium, which is good because it is all justices agreeing. Then you have to remember majority is. For instance, my opinion was a majority 7-1 with one dissent. No, I was not mad at the dissent because sometimes the dissent is another judge or judge[s]' opposite view from a legal standpoint. Clarence Thomas was 100% correct in my dissent. He spoke about not having a COA granted, and he also spoke about not raising the issue in the lower courts. He was exactly right and the way it was articulated made sense. People get caught up on the fact that it was a dissent but I did not. Any reasonable man would tell you he was right. You have to remember that when I went to the Supreme Court, I did not have a COA, nor did I have Johnson in the original petition, even though I tried to supplement it. You have to have it supplemented under the right rule in order for the courts to accept it. You have to remember that it is always up to the judge's discretion, depending what jurisdiction you're in. The Court of Appeals is 28 U.S.C. § 1291 or 18 U.S.C. § 3742 (guideline). The Supreme Court is 28 U.S.C. § 1254.

With Trump being the president, who knew what was going to happen. The A.U.S.A[8]. are always switched out when the president changes. Gwendolyn Stamper was replaced with John Alex Romano. Amir left to go fight in the court system against the ideas of Trump's executive orders. He told me Paul Smith left also to work at Georgetown. Amir once told me that in D.C. people change jobs all the time. He said, "Your friend from the office you go to Starbucks with one day could be working for a congressman or the president and then they give you the 'roll up the window effect.'" That was when they see you, they roll up the window and say, "I got to go, buddy, see ya." We started laughing.

Amir introduced me to another lawyer named James Dawson. When I first talked to John, the counselor was there for the call when he came on, he was not even fully registered yet in the eleventh circuit. I called Lyndsay and did my homework. She told me he was out of San Francisco and he clerked for Judge Alex Kozinski. I heard Kozinski was a tough judge to clerk for and he lasted so that means he was good. The first time we spoke privately, I told him that this was my life and if he was looking for something to just make a name off of that he could go. "I am living my case. When the phone hangs up,

---

[8] Trump fired Preet Bahara in NY, that was a bad mistake.

I am still in prison. I might die. I might stab someone, or get stabbed. This is my life," and he told me he understood, gave me his number, and told me to hit him up. I said, "Aiight." Amir told me he is going to another firm called Roderick & Solange MacArthur Justice Center. It was a nonprofit out of Minnesota or Chicago but had offices in D.C. They were a big organization that had a lot of different branches that helped people. The organization had offices all over the United States but they had a Criminal Appellate Division and a Supreme court Appellate Section. I figured they put Amir in charge because of his experience and his view(s) about social injustice. He is an excellent attorney. I would not trade the experience for anything in the world. Amir left for Rodrick and Solange in January of 2017. This time things were different. Amir told me he did not want to work where conflict of interest is the root. To limit the affiliation, it was like I lost my best friend. In February, Trump was in full swing. He rolled out the travel ban and that threw the airports into turmoil. Every lawyer was trying to make a name lined up, trying to be a solution to this grave injustice. Amir was front and center on the travel ban. Trump v. Hawaii is one example. That was when I understood the statement he made about him going to fight Trump. It was about challenging wrong public policy. It was about helping those that have been treated unjustly. I understood it then, what he was fighting for. The crazy part was, I would wonder how many people in prison actually were watching TV and knew of what was going on or was even affiliated to anyone making changes like that in society.

XXVII

When you are in federal prison, the strangest thing is that what happens in politics affects the federal prison system in some way. Keep in mind that the OIG9 is an agency that covers government misconduct. They are regulated by congress and the B.O.P receives funding from the United States government. When the travel ban was enacted, that trickled down to the borders. Immigration Custom Enforcement started to clamp down on the borders. When they did that, the prisons in California became overcrowded. Then they had to make space for the influx of people from South America. Within weeks I watched the feds turn to gangland, the spot I was in was not saturated that much, but they started sending people from Victorville, Atwater, Beaumont, and prisons out west. When I say out west for instance Victorville is a complex in Victorville, California. Atwater is in California also and Beaumont is Texas as well. Any prison that is west of Texas is considered "out west." Now if you do not know out West, Mexicans do no cell with Blacks, eat with them, nor even talk to them. I never understood that. The crazy part at the time, I was talking to a woman from San Diego, and she was telling me about it and my peeps out west would tell me through text about who got stabbed. Why they got stabbed. Most of it was for racism. I despise racism, all forms, whites hating blacks, Hispanics hating blacks, vice versa. Growing up in the South I have experienced it firsthand, not only from a subtle standpoint but a more direct one. Whereas it is blatant that the actions of the individual is nothing short of it. I think it is mostly people who are raised in fear or even pretending oppression is the alternative to not making a living. Being an immigrant or from a family of immigrants, I looked at life differently. I believed in hard work, I was raised with the belief if you don't have anything, at least come with respect. Bring something to the table, rather than two long empty hands.

XXVIII

After Amir left, James kept me updated through emails and legal calls which were always on point. It seemed as if he was very determined to win. He earned my respect. I started getting more and more cases to do. One day we were on lockdown when the Unit Manager pulled me out for legal mail and said, "Welch, why are you not getting any money for all these guys using your name? The ones using your name are blessed because of your Supreme Court case." I told him, "It is not about the money at this level." I was thinking, there is no price for talking to the many people who helped in making of the Welch Doctrine possible. He wished me well and said, "Alright." Don't get me wrong, I was making money not in the sense of getting it sent in, I was getting knowledge and experience for reading cases and writing letters to the courts of appeals in the form of 28(j) letters. 28(j) letters are based on the Federal Rule of Appellate Procedure 28(j), supplemental authority. You could only use 350 words. "That's it." They don't want to hear about any excuses. Just facts. That was cool, because most of the times the truth set you free, unless you pissed off somebody with political clout and you get aggressive lawyers that go hard. Then it is what it is.

XXVIV

I was introduced to someone by one guy, he was from Fort Myers. When I met him, I told him that I do not have time to take any new cases and he said that he knew me. I asked, "How you know me? Where you from?" He told me, "Fort Meyers." I said, "Yeah." Then he asked me where I was from! I told him that we would discuss that later. He said he was in the county jail hearing about the "Welch Doctrine." He said that I helped out one of his homeboys. I asked which one and he said, "Chicken." I said I knew Chicken. "He real burnt out" (burnt out means crazy) and walked like George Jefferson. "Right," he said. "Yeah, that's him." I said, "Yeah, that's him." He tried to talk about who I knew and I said, "Let's not go there, I will spin the track with you." Then we started to break his case down and show him what's going wrong, what angles to take and where we would go and how to give the time back. He asked me, "What hand do you write with?" I told him I was left-handed and he said, "I got a book I want you to read." It was Malcolm Blackwell's *David & Goliath*.

When I say it opened my eyes it's because it was like the book was talking to me. It spoke (no, I was not smoking either. I don't smoke.). It spoke about thinking from the left and overcoming obstacles. He sold me on that, then we spoke about Henry Louis Gates Jr. and a book called *100 Amazing Facts About the Negro*. That was an excellent book. It broke down the historical facts about Blacks throughout history and what they had to overcome and the significance of their role throughout history.

XXX

I started to think when it's all said and done, what would be my role through history and if I made any significant difference in history like that! I felt like I was not getting any notoriety. Notoriety was not significant to me what was significant was the fact that I was helping people and getting results that brought a feeling like no other. Then as I was walking one day with Twin, someone came up to me and gave me a hug and said, "My hero." Twin was shocked and said, "The man called you his hero, bro, that's deep." We continued walking, Twin said, "I got someone I want you to meet," he introduced to me one of his friends. Then his friend said, "You Welch?" He said, "Thee Gregory Welch v. United States?" I said, "Yes." He said, "I am officially glad to meet you because I heard good things about you in my last spot and a lot of people owe you." I said they went home. He said, "Some did, some got they time cut." I said, "That's what's up." Twin then said, "You do not believe how big you are." I said, "It's not about that. It's about your rights under the Constitution." I told him that I believed in the Constitution. I believe that it has the ability to change their condition or situation(s) as long as you believe. He talked about his case. I told him, "All you talk about is how they gave you 30 years, 'they set me up,' you're missing the point. In the feds, your case is never about you." I said, "You are the body to the number that is assigned to you." Then I told him, "It is bigger than you and me. Just take the time to think about it. When you see that, I will help you."

XXXI

The following day he asked to read something about me. I gave him an article from one of blogs. At lunchtime he gave it back to me and he wanted to see my work. I said, "Go on the computer and type in 'Welch v. United States 136 S.Ct. 1257 (2016).'" He said, "Are you a computer?" I said it's committed to memory. Then he said, "You have a lot of haters." (It was difficult for me to grasp why people would hate me for winning. I thought I would be congratulated, it did not turn out like that.) I said, "I must be successful." I had gotten my case records and gave it to him. He said, "Damn, that's a lot." I said that just the Supreme Court stuff, not the 2241, 2255, Rule 41, FOIA requests. He probably thought I was crazy. I did not see him for a couple of days. I had been busy putting my bond motion together. I had gotten a legal call, I told James I wanted to do a motion for a bond hearing this time. They had a case going before the Supreme Court called Stokeling v. United States (cert was not granted yet). I was skeptical about it because his priors were armed with the exception for one. I did not understand fully how that was going to work. I told James what I wanted to do and the rule that applied. I would say within a week or so, the motion was field. We filed the motion under Federal Rules of Appellate Procedure. Again it gave us jurisdiction to go back to the district court and file the motion. This time, I caught back up with Twin and he told me that he read my case and he said they denied me 15 times. I said, "You realized something." He asked, "What was that?" "I <u>never</u> gave up. I kept pressing on. Stayed in court, filed supplements and continued. You also forgot that nothing was <u>never</u> dismissed." He said, "Yeah," and that I go hard. He said if

I can file a supplement for him and I said I take my legal work seriously and he would have to spend some time in the law library with me because I would rather he have some knowledge about what's going on because I am not the type you throw paper on the desk and ask me to file for you. You have to understand what's going on at some point because you're going to get a lawyer and you have to know how to talk to them because once you know how to relay the issue he/she is going to break it down from their experience and legal understanding.

XXXII

Once you know how to communicate with the attorney, it makes it a lot easier, and it helps bridge gaps of misunderstanding. The average lawyer has not been locked up nor do they think about going to prison. They run from the idea of being locked up, so we as defendants have to learn to have empathy when an attorney lacks understanding unless they blatantly say or do something to show they're not interested. Time started going by. I told Twin that I needed to see his docket sheet[9] before I filed anything. Then he said he "don't have none." Then I asked for his paperwork, then he said he would have to order it. I said, "Alright." It took about two weeks. The lawyer sent his appeal briefs before we got the trial transcripts. I used the appeal briefs to file the motion to supplement. The court sent it back as unfiled, because we had a counsel on record. Then we filed a motion to relieve counsel after we filed that, the district court denied it.

---

[9] Docket sheet lists in order the events that take place within the jurisdiction of the case whether appeal or district court have different docket sheets.

XXXIII

We made a FOIA request to all the agencies involved in his case. In order to obtain any kind of relief in the courts, you have to have a strategy; a beginning strategy and an exit strategy. We started the issue(s) on Direct to build ground(s) for the 2255. While that was going on, I was filing second and successive petitions based on my case and they were getting granted. This time they had already denied my motion for bond. It was alright, but I do not like to go backwards. I felt I was not paying attention to my calling. This time the Supreme Court was arguing Sessions v. Dimaya. The name changed to Sessions because Jeffery B. Sessions was the Attorney General and he was bringing the fight to Dimaya (which was wrong because they kept Dimaya in custody while people were going home on his case, sound familiar?). Dimaya was talking about the residual clause in a statute called 18 U.S.C. § 16(b). They had to re-argue Dimaya because the judges were deadlocked in a 4-4 decision and at the time they only had 8 justices. The President chose Neil Gorsuch. It was a sigh of relief because he was a constitutionalist. Which is good because he believes the constitution was a living document, which is good at some times, other times, it might not be that good. It was alright, his confirmation was not full of controversy (a confirmation hearing is how Supreme Court Justices get to know if they get the job). The best confirmation was Ruth Bader Ginsburg 97-1, which was pretty good. It's like no one had anything bad to say. The confirmation process seems embarrassing because they display your life on national TV and treat you like everything wrong you did makes you the worst person in the world. If you find a perfect human being, please let me know. I want to shake his/her hands. He was confirmed. I liked some of his opinions about the 2241 Prost v. Anderson case because it was a good case and United States v. Silas came out of his circuit. He came from Colorado and Colorado is a part of the Tenth Circuit. The Tenth Circuit was a very liberal circuit. I understood why he did not have any problems being confirmed in the Supreme Court. At the time, a lot of people were upset with what was going on with the political climate in America. I understood it. People were fed up with politicians lying and making false promises. Trump installed a reality check in America. He told America, "This is who I am. Take it or leave it." As Malcolm X said, "I would rather you tell me who you are than call me names behind closed doors." America was set back, but I believe that it has to get worse before it gets better and America was at a moment of correction. A correction that was needed.

XXXIV

Justice Neil Gorsuch was confirmed, I asked an attorney that was familiar with the court. He said when he walked by Scalia's chair, it was turned around to signify that it is to be occupied. It's funny how simple things of that nature can let someone know to be prepared for change. Change I was prepared and ready for. At this point it seemed as if everyone on the compound had something to say about my case and something to say about how I write. You name it. I heard it. Everything from "I don't know what I am doing" to "I am asking people for help." The crazy part is I knew where it was coming from. I asked Unique, "would I be wrong to stab someone and send a message?" He said, "You came too far to go backwards. You work too hard to fall back." Then he said, "You are doing something right. That is where the hatred comes from. It is based on jealousy and jealousy is for suckers." He stated, "G, you grew on me. I used to walk with you and people would ask you for me, now they ask me for you. Push me out the way to talk to my brother. I love that about you. You see what you want and go for it." I told him I learned from the best. I had seen Twin, this time he came to me with a letter from the courts. It was clear he was upset. I took the letter from him. It was the response from the courts denying his motion to supplement. I looked at him and saw that he did not understand. I pulled out the paper and the contents from the envelope and said, "Can you understand what they said to you, besides denied?" He said, "No. They denied me." I told him, "That got you." He said, "Of course they got me, I am serving 30 years." I told him, "I am Gregory Welch v. United States of America 136 S.Ct. 1265, 1267 (2016)." A rule is substantive, rather than procedural, when it alters the range of conduct and it is unconstitutional for someone to be convicted of a crime that is no longer criminal. I then said, "1,342 people was the last amount I checked. Some are on their way back. Some would kill you for complaining to me about your fucking 30 years." Then I told him the Federal Rules of Criminal Procedure was enacted by Congress to catch gangsters and some gangsters' forces. "They had to change them, and you are complaining to me about your first denial." I shook my head and said, "Them people fucked you up and what are we going to do?" I said, "What are you going to do? Me? Then he said, "Come on, Welch." I told him, "You missing the point. The paper they gave you said more than denied, for instance where it says: 'In the Court of Appeals for the Eleventh Circuit Atlanta David J. Smith Clerk of Court,'

below it says your name and case number, then it says the reason for the denial, meaning explanation as to why it was denied. When it says that, below is the case handler's phone number then." He said, "Welch, you been doing this." I said, "No, we fighting for our life, the most important tool we have is comprehension. Once we have comprehension, then what's on paper is simple to master." Slowly but surely he started to understand what my mission was.

XXXV

Where the facility was located, we would take walks. Me and Twin became friends. He would ask me questions about the law. I was working the Leisure Law Library passing out magazines, so in the afternoons he would come out and ask what's next. I would explain to him about building a digital footprint. He would ask what it was. I would explain the significance of the Fifth Amendment of the U.S. Constitution and that due diligence is similar to a digital footprint. I would show him that everything we file gets docketed on a docket sheet. For example, D.E.1 and D.E.2 and once things get docketed, it gets admitted into the record and once it's into the record, it is proof that it was in litigation. He would ask, "How do you retain that information?" I would let him know that I read the law like an urban novel and that I read the constitution and I understand it. As time went on everything with my case started to slow down. The motion I was filing was certiorari. This time I was challenging the constitutionality of the habeas corpus because I won a 2241 in the Court of Appeals. It was Rivas v. Warden F.C.C. Coleman. It was a shock because the Eleventh Circuit denied McCarthen v. Goodwill Industries in March. I remember because the compound was buzzing saying the 2241 is no longer valid and that after McCarthen, it is dead to an extent. They were right. But dead wrong at the same time because McCarthen was an en banc decision and en banc decisions almost always overrules old existing law because there is sometimes a mistake in the previous panel decision. The panel in McCarthen overruled a lot of bad case law such as Wofford v. Scott Bryant v. Warden and Mackey v. United States. One problem the Eleventh Circuit had since I had been in was the fact that they had a lot of angry litigators, that obstruct people with valid issues because believe it or not, the courts answer the call when you call them out. When you jump out there without any facts, they check it real quick. I had two petitions in the Supreme Court this time, United States v. Bernard and United States v. Denmark. The justices ordered the Solicitor General to respond. I was having fun with the new Solicitor General because I kept sending the petitions to Michael Dreeban. Michael Dreeban was the Solicitor General in my case and the new Solicitor General was Noel J. Francisco from Jones Day in Washington, D.C. So I could imagine how upset he was when he kept seeing Michael Dreeban's name because at that time Michael Dreeban was being borrowed for the Trump investigation into the Russia meddling probe. To me, that was serious. However, this is not about politics. In United States v. Denmark, I questioned the retroactivity of Welch in a habeas corpus, that was a felony case. I knew the answer but wanted the Solicitor General to answer. Writing motions is like having an argument about a legal theory. Your point has to be proven with facts of law. He did not answer. He cited another case that his office wanted in the Supreme Court which was Untied States v. Wheeler from the Fourth Circuit. Wheeler won his 2241 and his conviction was vacated. The government was upset. They tried to cite McCarthen and the Fourth Circuit was not having it. They turned down the government and said that they were wrong and that McCarthen would not apply in the Fourth Circuit. That created a circuit capitalized on it and incorporated it into my motion. This time the courts have reargued Sessions v. Dimaya —U.S.— (2017). It went well from what the oral argument looked like. If the oral argument goes well it does not mean that the person or corporation won because believe it or not, the justices are sworn to secrecy and Supreme Court Justices are family. No matter how you look at it. They stick together. I had a strong feeling he got it because the government tried to switch positions on what they were saying about the residual clause of the 18 U.S.C. § 16(b) and that did not make any sense.

XXXVII

This time I started teaching Twin about the Sixth Amendment and the confrontation clause, the jury trial, plain error and harmless error. It was hard because when I stepped outside my housing Unit people were always asking legal questions. Some days were good, and some were bad. The food was not bad, the only time it would be bad was when the fiscal year ended in September and the kitchen would not have much good food. Either it was stolen, or they just simply did not have enough, and we were fed on an alternate meal. I was constantly thinking about my children. My mom wanted me to sign over custody to her and I was upset because I felt like she was taking my babies away.

My kids were always my world. I would wonder how they were doing. Mom would tell me they were house kids and were boring. All they did was "sleep and eat" and they would "read and watch TV on they phone." I have to say they were alright. My son was the one I was more concerned about because he was black and driving. I would worry about getting that phone call one day and that is something all parents don't want to hear, he was at the age where he was trying to prove he was a man and I felt he was so far away from it because he never showed that he was willing to challenge the status quo. I always felt that something was wrong but I could not put my finger on it. I checked their report cards and helped them with homework, keep updates on field trips, send them pictures, wallets, pocketbooks, things to let them know I am thinking about them.

From time to time, they would tell me that they remembered the things we used to do together, and they knew we were going to be back together. My mother really held me down and for that I would be forever grateful. I promised her that I would fight my case and do the right thing. It was not easy all the time. There were ups and downs.

Through this experience, I learned that humility and perseverance are very important. Humility because it helps to keep me grounded. Sometimes talking to me, people would think I am arrogant. That is far from the truth, I am confident about the things I learned and very grateful for the experience. Perseverance played a significant role because being denied when you are right is very difficult. Especially when you have that actual gut feeling that you are right.

The Supreme Court ruling in Sessions v. Dimaya. It was a plurality opinion. Plurality opinions means that one justice was a deciding vote (they look like this: 4-1-4 with the indecisive justice making a concurring opinion or a dissenting opinion). I like Justice Gorsuch's separate opinion because he was getting in depth with his thoughts about the actual reading in the slip op. Slip op means slip opinion; it is not yet fully published and there may or may not be corrections once completed. J. Gorsuch stated:

"Vague laws invited arbitrary power. Before the revolution, the crime of treason in English Law was so capaciously construed that the mere expression of disfavored opinions could invite transportation or death. The founders cited the crown's abuse of 'pretended' crimes like this as one of their reasons for revolution" (Slip Op.1).

Reading that gave me a moment of clarity that there might be a silver lining because to me that made me think that his views on the law were that an individual shouldn't be punished for a statute that does not have sufficient clarity. He even went further when on page 4 stated: "unless an offense [was] set forth with clearness and certainty." The indictment risked being held void in Court Id. at 302 (emphasis deleted); ZW. Hawkings, pleas of the crown, Ch. 25 §§ 99, 100, pp. 244-245 (2d.Ed. 1726). These were ancient cases before the antebellum period I discussed earlier. The value in them was the fact they spoke about how the constitution was drafted, how the founders' views of an injustice was not right. Please don't construe what I am saying as I am taking sides. Associate Justice did an excellent job on the opinion. The direction I had seen the court going was, they were going to challenge the residual clause of the § 924(c)(3)(B) because in the opinion, separate opinion and the dissent spoke clearly that "any" statute with "in the course of" "in furtherance of" invite arbitrary enforcement. I knew that phrase all too well. Justice Kennedy wrote about it in my opinion but he clarified the standards of what constitutes retroactivity. For instance, he stated:

"A rule is substantive rather than procedural if it alters the range of conduct or the class of persons that the law punishes" (Welch quoting Schrior, 542 U.S. 353). "This includes decisions that narrow the scope of a criminal statute by interpreting its terms, as well as constitutional determinations that place particular conduct or persons covered by the statute beyond the states' power to punish" (Slip op. 8 (Slip opinion, page 8)). My opinion was the standard 15 pages. Could you imagine 15 pages can take someone serving a life sentence and bring them back to life?

I am thankful to be blessed with the opportunity to write. Welch Doctrine is not fully about Welch v. United States, it is just a small view as to what was going on, during brief moments of the author's life what motivated him to move forward, how he used his talent to gain success and help hundreds if not hundreds of thousands of people, scholars, and laymen. Hopefully. Enjoy.

There is no feeling to explain how that feels. I could imagine how that feels. In prison you can look in someone's eyes and see despair. It is like someone is literally walking dead. In prison (federal prison), life means life. That means when you are dead, your sentence is over. 10 years means you do 85% of your sentence. The experience was a learning experience. I cannot replace the years lost, the family members that passed away. The best lessons I learned was humility, patience, gratitude, willingness, honesty, caring, objectivity, responsibility, open-mindedness. Believe it or not, these are words that they have in the housing units. I do not know if people ever take the time to read them. Me, I read almost everything when I can, I learned that from reading *Man's Search for Meaning* by Viktor Frankel. Books like that helped to give me a broader sense of my reality, that things could be a lot worse than what I was going through. Learning the law is not an easy task because you have to understand how to apply what you know in the right procedure. You have to understand sentence structure, and the significance of circuit precedents.

XXXVIII

After I started helping Twin it became an uphill battle. Not only from the compound, but his judge and getting the transcripts from the court. Whenever you file "any" motion in court you have to read what's going on with the case. Some cases, for instance small claims or some civil litigations, you can get good enough information from either party; however, it is best to read the transcripts (take notes) to write an effective brief. As the months passed I kept thinking when were they going to file their final brief. Around this time I got a better understanding of my new attorney. He was a young Yale graduate that went to Columbia University in Manhattan and taught a former inmate who got out and graduated from Yale. He would tell me how I remind him of him but I actually won and that I keep going. He was a good person from time to time. He would ask what drove me. I would tell him, my kids over and over again. I continued to fight, I started meeting more attorneys who either knew me or knew of the situation. I felt as if I had a microscope on me at all times and it felt uncomfortable because I am a low-key person. There were times when people would always say that I pass them every day or they did not know my name. I do like my privacy and I am a very private person. One of the most important duties of an attorney is privacy. You have to know how to keep your mouth shut no matter what some of the things you read and come across, you have to be able to not say anything nor be careless.

Working on Twin's case was similar to mine. Not with the statutes, but the complexity of the litigation. There was evidence withheld, no transcripts and it was almost impossible to get in contact with the attorney. I filed a complaint with the Bar (only to find out his colleagues wrote statements in his behalf). We then filed a FOIA request only to be denied in every stage.

The system is designed to break you down in every shape and form. The worst is mentally. The mental aspect starts when you become sentenced. You begin to wonder what's next, then when you figure out what's next, then comes how, the irony is when you finally get your footing. You have to figure out how you're going to keep going without losing your ground.

XXXIV

I have seen in plenty of guys facing the what next! Or "how do I fight?" I have seen guys give up. Some commit suicide, resort to homosexuality, or live under a pretense of who they are not. It is in no way, shape or form, easy. That's not including the various pitfalls that are in place. For instance, gangs, drugs, gambling, extortion, conmen. In federal prison, it's like they take the best of the best in the criminal world and the worst of the worst. Believe it or not, you learn to maneuver. Once you figure out how you are going to do your time, then everything falls into place. It started for me in the penitentiary, I realized my freedom and my integrity is worth more than anything. I believed respect is earned and the simplest things can carry the most significant value. The cases I do I was using the Constitution, mainly the Fifth Amendment. I use that Amendment because it is not confusing and once you start to break down the issue, it turns into a simple granted or denied. I do not believe in giving my enemies ammunition to harm me. Case in point, keep it simple, less is best. Once I pass the Bar, then I am going to change legislature, by focusing on what is needed.

Sometimes the days in prison are slow but for the most part once you keep yourself busy, time flies. For instance, when you have a prison job, it builds discipline because believe it or not, you have to be there and most prison jobs offer a skill. For instance, UNICOR teaches industrial experience. Food Service teaches food preparation, food management, how to cook, store, and maintain food. Laundry teaches about how to operate a laundromat. Then they have sanitation, commissary retail sales, Medical, hospital orderly, Psychology

Mental Health, Library librarian, Education, a tutor, teacher, learn a trade, compound, facilities, R&D Receiving and Discharge. Believe it or not every department has a job, but not every department hires frequently based on your skill. Most likely you will find a job. I mostly worked in Education, Psychology, Suicide Watch and a Mental Health Companion. I liked to genuinely help people. It is a drain sometimes but I feel that was my calling.

As I started getting the results I was fighting for, it left me with a question mark as what next to do and how to go about it. I started taking college courses so when I get out I can continue my education. I did not want to take a paralegal course because I want to be an attorney, not a paralegal. However that was the wrong way to think about it because paralegals are the backbone to "ANY" type of law office. I started off doing Sociology first. That was pretty good, it opened my eyes to the different social classes of the world and different people. Then I started realizing that Blacks in prison were disenfranchised severely.

XXXX

It is September 2018 now. The time had flown by. I was working suicide watch and this particular time it was a busy day. It is busy when there are constant disruptions by the person on suicide watch, sometimes the people would be getting ready to get transferred then they act up to try and stay. This time things seemed off, the officer working was cool did not bother no one. The person I was watching kept blocking the window I was trained to pay attention to. I was trained to pay attention to both sides of the room. As I was paying attention to the individual I was watching, the officer on the other side went to grab a sharp object from the person in the room. Then the individual grabbed the officer. I used the phone and called control. Within 2 minutes the area I worked was flooded with officers. They were surprised when they asked who pressed the button.

XXXXI

I was rewarded for the act of heroism as they called it. I did not care for the money they gave me I just wanted to go home. I wanted the nightmare to end and I wanted to be free, days in prison are very dark and lonely no matter how you try to make it seem alright the more and it would suck in you into despair. I did not help the officer for notoriety I did it because we had taken classes in there that taught about hostage situations and what to do when things get drastic. I just did what I was trained to do. In December of that same year, Trump signed into law the FIRST STEP ACT. It was a sigh of relief because it changed the 100:1 ratio and made the crack law retroactive. Of the people that obtained relief, there were people who had life sentences that were given a second chance. After that I saw guys finally start to wake up because there were people that were left behind from Obama. The FIRST STEP ACT gave people a second chance who had long draconian drug sentences. The FIRST STEP ACT changed the compassionate release provision of the 18 USC 3582, it was a blessing because that is what I would use to get out of prison.